The Little Book of Collectable British PYREX

Susan McGowan studied at the Dorset Institute of Higher Education before being awarded a BA at Southampton University. After almost a decade as an Internal Auditor in the Civil Service, and twenty years as a school librarian, Susan now devotes herself to reading, researching and writing.

The Little Book of Collectable British PYREX

Susan McGowan

'Pride of England' Casserole Dish

©Susan McGowan 2019

This book is sold subject to the condition that it shall not, by way of trade or otherwise, be lent, resold, hired out, or otherwise circulated without the publisher's prior consent in any form of binding or cover other than that in which it is published and without a similar condition including this condition being imposed on the subsequent publisher.

The moral right of Susan McGowan has been asserted.

ISBN 9781999932145

First published in Great Britain in 2006
By The Diggory Press

3nd edition 2018
Butterfly Cottage Publishing
87 Shalmsford Street, Chartham, Kent

Introduction

PYREX was patented in America in 1915, and the name PYREX is still a registered trademark of Corning Incorporated. PYREX glass was produced in the UK, under licence, between 1921 and 1973 by the company James A. Jobling. Having been made only during this limited period of 52 years, it is becoming increasingly rare and collectable.

This book is a first attempt to catalogue the vast range of British PYREX shapes and patterns still in circulation.

I would like to thank all the collectors of PYREX who have sent me pictures and stories, and all the eBay sellers who have allowed me to use their photographs. Special thanks go to Dorothy and Raymond Hunter for sharing their photographs, and to Geoff Parkhouse for his support and encouragement. I would also like to thank the editors of, and contributors to, *'Mixed Batch'*, the Jobling house magazine, whose work I have pored over at length – it's fascinating stuff!

I hope you all find as much enjoyment as I did in discovering the history behind one of our most common household items.

Contents

A Brief History of the Jobling Glassworks   1
Production Methods……………………………..   8
Shapes and Sets …………………………………...   12
Colours ….…………………………………………..   19
Patterns. ……………………………………………   22
Design Directory…………………………………..   24
Marks and Labels..………………………………….   88
JAJ Collectables…………………………………….   92
Commemorative Ware ……………………….   102
Working at the Jobling Factory ……………….   104

A Brief History of the Jobling Glassworks

In 1858 Angus and Henry Greener started the Wear Flint Glass Works in Sunderland, but the works did not prosper, and in 1885 they were taken over as a bad debt by James Augustus Jobling, owner of the Tyne Oil and Grease Works in Newcastle.

It was at about this time that a new discovery in glass making had been made in America. The firm of Corning were looking into problems posed by the railroad companies. The lanterns on trains often caused trouble when the glass globes cracked, owing to stress caused by differences in temperature between the flame and any ice or snow, which collected on it. Corning's eventually produced a special heat-resisting borosilicate glass, which was ideal for the lanterns. This was the birth of PYREX cookware.

People at the time thought it was only suitable for lamp glasses and laboratory ware, until (so the story goes) one of the laboratory workers cut the bottom off a PYREX jar, took it home and asked his wife to test it in her oven as cookware. It was a hugely successful experiment, and PYREX glass is still used in our kitchens today.

James Jobling's nephew, Ernest Jobling Purser, joined the firm in 1902, and in 1921 he persuaded the company to acquire the patent rights for the production of a heat resistant glass in 'Great Britain and the Empire (excluding Canada)', which included Great Britain & Ireland, Australia, New Zealand, South Africa, India and Egypt. The original plain casseroles were an immediate success, and in quick succession many new types and styles of dishes were added.

Pie dishes of all sizes, fruit sets and eventually complete dinner sets were all manufactured in clear PYREX glass. Many dishes were sold with silver-plated holders so that they would not look out of place at the dinner table.

To begin with, PYREX products were marketed as labour saving and energy-saving. One 1930s advert (left) even gave a chart showing how much cooking time could be saved by using PYREX cookware.

The advert also points out the 'delicate pale-gold tinge' of the PYREX dishes, which would match the housewife's existing crystal or tinted glass items. This distinctive colour, arising from impurities in the glass, was later eliminated, leaving PYREX glass clear and sparkling.

One of the main advantages of PYREX glass, and an innovation at the time, was the fact that food could be cooked and served in the same dish, thus keeping it warm on the way to the table. This was especially useful to housewives during the war years.

The advert on the right shows how to make rations go further by using PYREX cookware. All PYREX glass came with a guarantee against oven-heat breakage.

By 1949, when Ernest Jobling Purser retired, the original half-acre works had increased to six acres, and the workforce had increased from 250 in 1922 to over 1,350.

In 1951, John D. Cochrane joined the company as a designer, and later rose to be Company Director. This was a golden period for Jobling, as Britain recovered from the austerity of the war years. Technological improvements abounded, and the modern housewife clamoured for bright, new designs.

Mr Cochrane

In 1952, Jobling introduced Flameware skillets and saucepans and, in May of the same year, the first coloured PYREX ware was launched, which was also an immediate success.

September 1953 saw a push in advertising PYREX glassware to the housewife. The 'Spearhead' campaign addressed this need, as dealers across the country were sent cartons containing six of the most popular and reasonably priced ovenware lines, a small free gift, a window bill, stickers for each piece, and new price lists to pass on to the customer.

The Spearhead packs in production, 1953.

Opalware was introduced in 1954. This was a glass that could be heated and then plunged into cold water and was almost unbreakable. The company made tableware for hospitals and other catering establishments.

Caterware was also produced for use in company canteens, so it is often possible to find items showing a company logo. It was so successful that before long it was re-designed and re-named Tableware. During this period, the Jobling six-acre site expanded to an enormous forty acres. By 1955 the workforce stood at 2,400.

In the late 1950s, Corning developed a product called Pyroceram, which further resisted breaking and chipping. The body was solid white, and did not have the translucency of Opalware, being more akin to ceramic than glass. This was produced by Jobling as Pyrosil from the 1960s, with an aggressive marketing campaign that claimed the dish would 'almost wash itself' after frying boiling or casseroling. Lucky buyers could be entered into a prize draw for the chance to win a £1,000 dream kitchen.

Pyrosil jugs and dishes came with a blue flower design on it, and has attracted its own following of collectors. On the right is a tiny promotional plastic fridge magnet measuring just 2" across.

Although Jobling had begun making headlamp glasses and traffic signal lenses in the 1930s, by 1960 the factory was concentrating solely on glasses like PYREX and Pyrosil. Every piece of British PYREX tableware ever produced has been made in Sunderland. It is reported that in the period 1946-1958 Jobling production of PYREX® domestic wares increased by 94%.

Many changes were seen during the development of the Jobling factory, not least in the transport and distribution of PYREX glass In the September 1955 edition of Jobling's house magazine, a Mr Kettle recalls that 'The earliest days of our Transport Department will be remembered, perhaps with some regret, by our older employees, who can recall watching Jimmy Curtis' horse-drawn cart pull away from the gantry with sparks, froth and language flying - indeed a fearsome sight!' At the time of writing, the department ran 13 diesel vehicles to deliver their product.

New yellow and red van design introduced in 1957, featuring the Coronet design on a cup and saucer

The house magazine of 1961 describes three glass factories on one site in Sunderland at this time, another factory at Pallion (Sunderland), and subsidiary companies at Fenton and Stone (Staffs). There were warehouses at Heywood (Lancs.), West Chirton, and Colnbrook (Slough). There were 2,700 employees at the company, making it the largest employer in the Tyne & Wear area after the shipbuilding yards. The Decorating Department reports that ten million pieces of Opal glassware were produced and decorated in nine months that year.

A huge display of PYREX glassware in Dingles of Plymouth

PYREX ware continued to grow in popularity during the 1960s and 1970s, becoming a regular on wedding lists across the country. However, in 1973, Jobling's licence expired and Corning took over control of the company, ending the era of Jobling PYREX glass.

Production Methods

Early PYREX glass was produced as clear glass only, either pressed or mould blown but by the end of the 1920s the plain glassware was embellished. Many of the clear casserole and serving dishes had EPNS stands for use on the dining table, and early adverts focussed on the energy-saving and time-saving features of PYREX glass, rather than its decorative qualities.

The first methods used to decorate PYREX glassware were the traditional skills of engraving and cutting, which were applied after the piece was made.

Engraved gravy boat and stand

In the 1930s, Jobling started to press mould items, which was a cheaper method of production, being less labour-intensive. One of the first patterns produced by this method was the Willow Pattern design. This was produced as a clear item for several years, before the introduction of a blue enamel to highlight the design.

This was quickly followed by the first Jobling designs produced by the transfer printing method. An engraved copper plate was used to transfer the design to the finished glassware, which was then fired to fix the pattern. The first two designs produced in this way were the blue Willow Pattern and the Avon pattern.

For a few years at the end of the 1930s, Jobling decorated clear PYREX ware with a double line of green enamel, applied with the use of a turntable, although this procedure was halted at the beginning of the Second World War in 1939.

Another innovation introduced just before the war, and consequently put on hold, was the development of a spray system to colour PYREX glassware. After the war, this system of spraying enamel onto the outside of the glassware by hand was perfected. However, it was not until 1952 that a full range of tableware was introduced, and by this time only the smaller pieces were hand-sprayed. Each piece of PYREX glass was inspected by hand as it came off the production line.

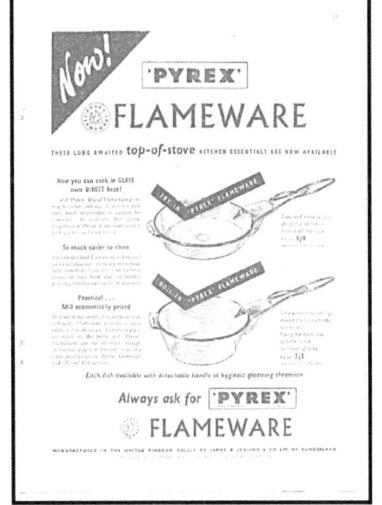

In 1938, Jobling started to produce Flameware glass frying pans and saucepans. Each set came with a detachable handle and had a blue tinge to it, to distinguish its use. Advertisements emphasised the fact that food could be cooked on the hob, and served in the same dish, which kept food hotter.

The Mixed Batch house magazine of September 1952 gives details of the various methods employed by Jobling for transferring a pattern to the glass body. It describes the Copper Plate process, whereby an engraver puts the design onto a copper plate, which is used to transfer the enamel design onto thin rice paper. The enamel is then pressed on the glass, and the paper is washed away. This was used for patterns like Blue Willow, Indian Tree and Old Castles.

Harlech Castle design in pale blue on a rounded Easy-Grip Opal base

The white body of Opal tableware is the PYREX glass that we are most familiar with, and which is most collectable. It was introduced in 1957, and signalled an explosion in decorative PYREX tableware and kitchenware.

The most effective method of decorating the clean white body of Opalware was screen-printing, and during the 1960s the shape of PYREX ware changed to meet the needs of this production method. A new range of flat-sided casserole dishes was introduced, which could easily accept the multiple layers of colour that were required for designs such as Chelsea. Jobling also mixed production methods, layering screen prints on top of sprayed grounds, as in the Gaiety and Hawthorn ranges.

As the Sixties progressed, more intricate designs were created, which required further developments in production methods. In fact, more than twenty-five new designs were introduced, and the company started to buy in sheets of screen printed and lithographic transfers.

During 1961, Jobling produced and decorated 600 pieces of dinner-ware for the Worshipful Livery of Glass Sellers in London.

Although border patterns were applied directly onto plates and casserole dishes, many designs were printed onto decal sheets, which were then applied after manufacture. The thick enamel of the screen-printed designs (e.g. June Rose) had a distinctive gloss appearance and a slightly raised surface, while the lithographic designs (e.g. Autumn Glory) had a more matte surface. Both these designs were fired after application to fix them.

Transfers continued to be bought in until the late 1960s and were popular with the company because unskilled workers could apply them. Towards the 1970s, however, Jobling decided to concentrate on designs they could produce themselves, such as Chelsea and Checkers.

Shapes and Sets

Jobling's PYREX ware was at the forefront of design, and won many awards from The Design Council. The basic shapes of the items changed to fit the demands of the housewife and the styles of the times. Many of these were inspired innovations and had an influence on the way we cook today.

The first English PYREX designs were introduced during the period of austerity after the First World War, and are known as Utility Ware. The designs reflect the mood of the times, being clean and unfussy. They all featured the trademark shaped handle on top of the lid, as shown on this individual  soup pot (right). This super little 7oz pot is marked with the JP logo and the code 500. It was sold in pairs.

The Streamline casserole range was introduced in 1931 and was rounder, without the raised handles. The lid was flat, so it could be used as another cooking or serving dish. These curvier designs were easier to produce, and easier for the housewife to clean – a winner all round! These were available in round, oval or octagonal shapes.

Streamline Oval Casserole Dish

The first full dinner service was offered in 1935, which extended the range from cookware to tableware. A 26-piece set included six dinner plates, six dessert plates, six side plates, two oval dishes, two casserole dishes and a sauceboat with matching stand. Even at this early stage, Jobling offered a one-year guarantee against breakage caused by damage from oven heat.

The Streamline designs were phased out during the war, as were the designs with knobbed lids. Soon after this, the opposing curve handles style was developed, which continued until the 1960s. In this design, the handles on the base and cover curved in opposite ways to make removal easier and safer.

Advert for Easy-Grip style Casserole Dish

In 1953, the Easy-Grip casserole range was introduced, giving the housewife a choice of square, oval or round casserole dishes in a variety of sizes. The range was marketed as giving the housewife 'everything you need for preparing, cooking, chilling, storing and serving', mentioning that PYREX glass 'cooks and looks better, makes washing-up easier. The wider handles were heralded as an innovation in design, protecting the housewife with 'safer, surer lifting and carrying'. A 2½ pint Easy-grip square casserole cost 10s 9d, as did the rectangular general-purpose dish. The soufflé dish that was brought out and marketed at the same time was also 2½ pint, and retailed for six shillings. Oval casserole dishes came in 1½, 2½ and 4 pint sizes, while the round ones were 8oz, 1 pint, 2 pint and 3 pint. The designs were typified by a generous rounded shape to the base, and cup and jug designs mirrored this rounding. Part of the range was a distinctive 'jockey cap' bowl, with a one-sided, integral handle.

These Easy-Grip casserole dishes were awarded a Council of Industrial Design Certificate in 1957, as being 'one of twelve products of outstanding design exhibited during the year'.

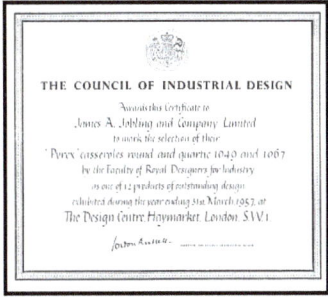 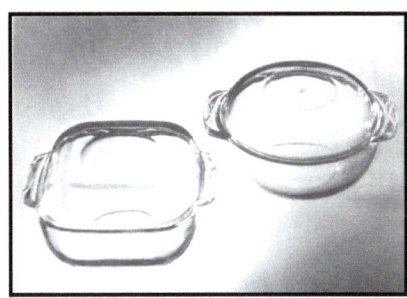

Easy-Grip dishes were later coloured with blue, red, green or yellow enamel on an Opal ground.

Casseroles were offered in 1 pint, 2 pint or 3 pint sizes at 4s 3d, 6s 6d and 8s 9d respectively. The new style pudding basins were introduced at this time, too, in 1, 1½ and 2½ pints, priced at 2s, 2s 9d and 3s 9d. The rolling pin with plastic ends joined this set of preparation tools.

By the end of 1958, Jobling were offering 127 items in their PYREX glassware range, in both clear and coloured designs, including three shapes and seven sizes of casserole dishes, ten different types of dishes and platters and ten complete dinner services.

With changes to modern living in the 1960s, tastes changed and the smooth, rolling curves of the Easy-Grip range were superseded by the straighter shapes of the Space Saver

Range. Handles became squarer, cup sides straightened and soup bowls with wide rims replaced the jockey-cap bowls of the 1950s. The meat platter, which had rounded corners, also acquired a new squarer shape.

Oddly enough, this period also saw the introduction of the mixing bowl with flared pouring lips, which doubled as handles. A complete set is quite hard to find.

Part of the Space Saver design range was also a set of mini-dishes sold in sets of six, which could be used for serving, or as stands.

The rounded butter dish (right) was introduced in 1972.

Jobling also introduced a set of three casserole dishes with straight sides that were narrower and deeper than previous designs, seen above with the June Rose design printed on them.

The triangular Serv-It dish (below) was introduced in 1979. This is after Corning took over the works, but many of the patterns were still produced in this shape, and the unusual design is very collectable. They were sold in sets of three.

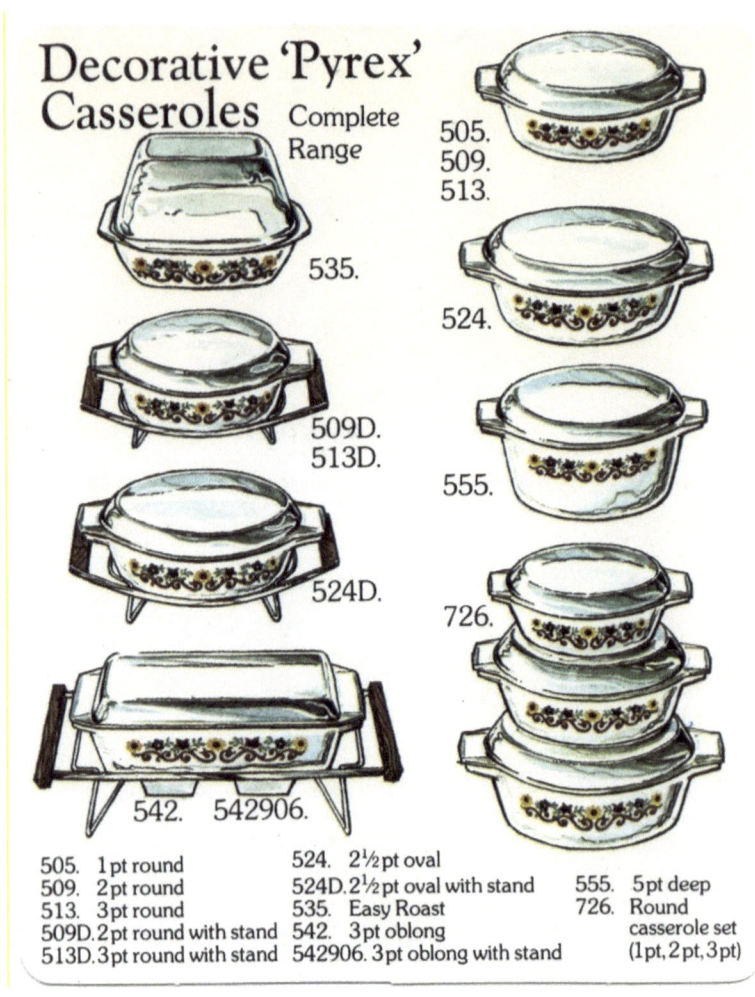

PYREX Space Saver Casserole Dish Shapes

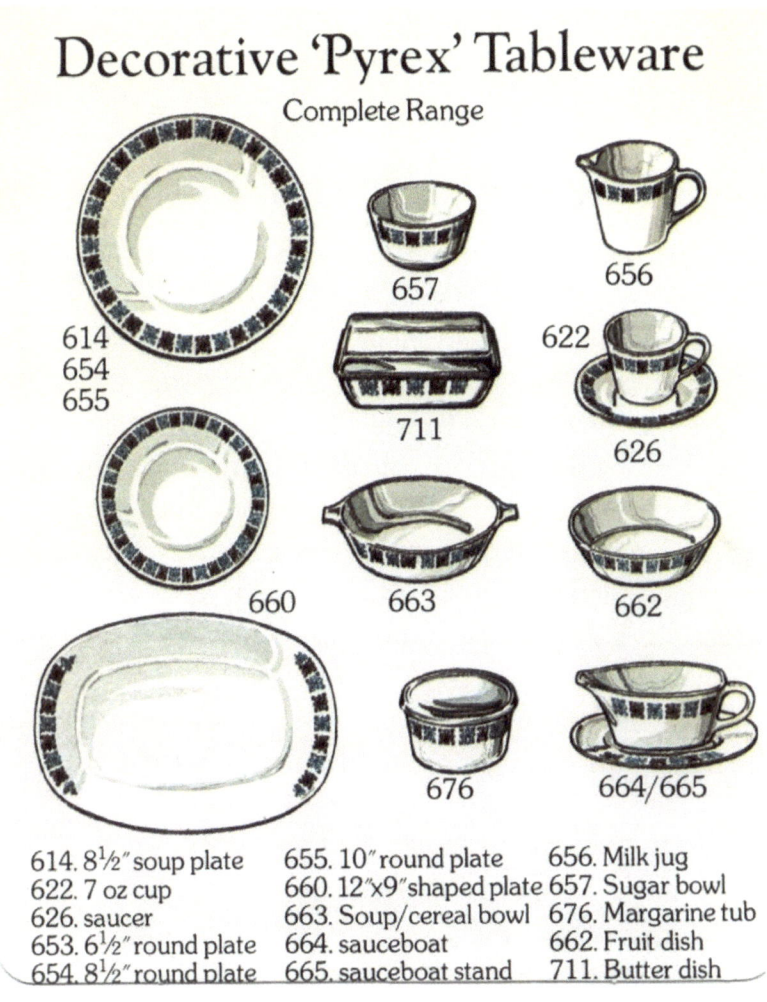

PYREX Space Saver Tea and Dinner Service Shapes

Colours

The first PYREX glassware was made in clear glass only and has the distinctive Vaseline or golden hue of 1920s glass. As time went on, the process was refined and PYREX glass became perfectly clear at the beginning of the 1950s.

Sprayware was introduced in 1939 in a choice of Jade Green, Powder Blue or Canary Yellow. At this time, there was no red as it was difficult to produce, but it was introduced later on, in 1957. These colours were withdrawn during the war, as were the engraved and cut designs, and they did not reappear until 1952, under the name Colourware. Champagne items, in a rich browny-cream, were also produced for a short time and were marketed as a 'restful' colour 'carefully chosen to tone with plain and coloured cloths or with the use of mats on any type of dining table'. The enamel was sprayed by hand onto each item.

Yellow and green gravy boats with matching stands.

Colourware items were produced when colour was sprayed onto the outside or underside of each item, leaving the surface, which would come in contact with food, as plain glass. Because the colour was seen through clear glass, it appeared bright and glossy.

A 25-piece set comprised six side plates, six sweet plates, six large dinner plates, one platter, two casseroles (four dishes altogether), sauceboat and stand. A plain set at this time was 66s 3d, while a coloured set was £1 12s 6d.

Part of the range was a set of coloured bowls, given the name Harlequin Set, which consisted of green (large), yellow (medium) and blue (small) bowls, presented in a gift pack, which cost 24s 3d in 1955. These three colours also featured on the fruit sets, and refrigerator dishes, which appeared in green (large), blue (medium) and yellow (small). The fruit sets contained one large bowl and six matching dishes, which were sold at 23s when they were first introduced.

Sadly, it was very easy to scratch the colour, as it was on the surface that was handled most often. It is rare to find pieces that have the enamel completely undamaged.

Opalware was the trade name given to PYREX glass produced in a clear bright white, which was most effectively used as a background for the strong, coloured designs that were introduced in the last thirty years of manufacture. Initially, tea and dinner sets were produced with no decoration, and these became known as Caterware, because of their commercial use.

In time, colour was sprayed onto the outside of the opal base (as with Sprayware) to produce the Weardale range, but innovations in transfer and screen-printing techniques led Jobling to favour these methods of decoration and most Opalware sported banded or decal designs. In 1957, Jobling was using 200,000 transfers a week. These designs, intended for domestic use, were lighter than the Caterware equivalents.

Tea sets were sold boxed in sets of eighteen pieces: six cups, six saucers and six tea plates.

Autumn Glory tea set with sugar bowl, jug and margarine tub

Patterns

Jobling employed a team of designers to ensure that their patterns were at the forefront of current fashions, and they showed regularly at Olympia.

Understanding the referencing of the numbers stamped into PYREX ware is a difficult job. In their sales catalogues, Jobling identified their patterns using reference numbers. These often (but not always) corresponded to the mould numbers. Letters often refer to designs, e.g. S for Streamline, W for Willow pattern. Mould numbers are sometimes suffixed by B for base and C for cover. On items produced after 1962, six-figure numbers were introduced. The first 3 numbers identify shape, the last three the style of decoration.

These are the numbers used for the main pattern designs:

000 – clear
001 – Colourware Dresden Blue
002 – Colourware green
003 – Colourware red?
004 – Colourware yellow
013 – Cloverleaf (on jugs)
120 – Gaiety black snowflake
122 – Gaiety white on turquoise daisy
127 – Matchmaker
128 – June Rose
130 – Weardale Deep Coral
134 – Chelsea
140 – Weardale Duck Egg Blue
144 – Checkers

146 – Hunting Scene
150 – Weardale yellow?
200 – Wheatsheaf
206 – Harvest Spray
260 – Pyrex Royal
261 – White Hawthorn on Claret ground
262 – White Hawthorn on green ground?
263 – White Hawthorn on Azure Blue ground
270 – Classics in Charcoal Grey
501 – Harvest
502 – Hunting Scene
503 – Wildfowl
504 – Fiesta
513 – 2001 flower design
516 – Kent Orchard
527 – Autumn Glory
528 – Cottage Rose
534 – Market Garden
562 – Sunflower
666 – Tuscany

A detailed list of items and their associated numbers can be found in the appendix.

Design Directory

2001

This was a fab and funky design for the Flower Power age, available in Turquoise or Orange, with a sprayed base and screen-printed lid. It was called the '2001' because it was guaranteed to last into the 21st century, and appeared on Space Saver casserole dishes, sold with a stand sporting trendy teak handles. It is unusual amongst PYREX casserole designs in that it had an opaque lid.

Turquoise '2002' numbered 513D-601

'2001' Casserole dish in Orange

Autumn Glory

This floral decal shows a large yellow flower, medium terracotta flowers and small white flowers arranged in a spray, with green leaves around the yellow flower. It was introduced in the 1960s and was described by Jobling as: 'Brilliantly burnished colours that bring a rich reminder of nature into the home.' Autumn Glory was produced using the lithographic transfer method, which gave a matte appearance to the pieces, but enabled the designer to make use of more subtle gradations in tone. Autumn Glory was produced on the Space Saver design opalware, and the design on smaller items, such as jugs and teacups, is a reduced version of the main design. This design was widely available on tea and dinner services, casserole dishes and mixing bowls. Jobling also produced matching items like melamine table mats and ash trays.

The complete Autumn Glory design (above) and the reduced design used on smaller items, such as sugar bowls (left)

An ash tray with Autumn Glory design

Autumn Glory casserole dishes and eared bowls

Melamine stands were produced in both oval and round shapes.

Avon

This border pattern was introduced in 1936 and was available in green or brown. It is very much like the borders available on ceramic tableware. Customers could buy a complete 26-piece dinner service packed in a box, or select individual items to purchase separately.

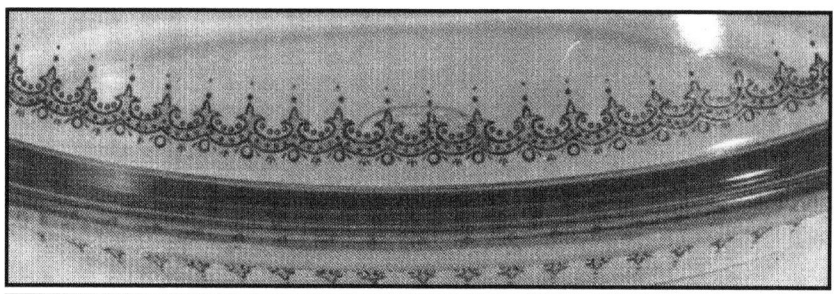

Baking Sets

These were the epitome of the PYREX oven-to-table dream, providing individual portions piping hot in pretty bowls. They were also used for serving snacks at the buffet table and were produced for a short while in bolder primary colours. These little sets with their matching pots and bent-wire stand have become one of the most collectable PYREX items of recent times. Available at first in pale Turquoise Blue, Primrose Yellow, and Pink, darker colours were introduced later on, with coral red replacing the pink. They carry the identification number 2186.

Baking Sets were presented in several different boxes. These are just two of them.

Briarwood

Briarwood design, described by Jobling as: 'A little artistic licence applied to a splendid tangle of wild roses makes this design a wonderfully vibrant table centre-piece.' Produced in the 1970s on Space Saver opalware, this design really was a sign of the times with its red, purple and orange colourway. It was available on mixing bowls and casserole dishes but not on tableware. For a short time, it was marketed as part of a Duo Set, comprising a 2pt and a 3pt casserole dish, with a free individual casserole in clear glass.

The Briarwood design on a Space Saver casserole dish

Checkers

This bold geometric design in blue and green was brought out in the 1960s is now very popular with collectors in Japan, but is not so sought after in the UK. It is interesting to note that this design was altered to fit on to different sized pieces – the large casserole had a much larger variation of the design than smaller pieces. The design was produced on Space Saver tea and dinner sets, casserole dishes and mixing bowls.

Casserole dish showing the larger printing of the design. The gravy boat is missing its stand. Boxed Checkers tea set (left).

Chelsea

This popular design consists of teal and black stylised flowers alternating in a block pattern. Introduced in the late 1960s, this design was described by Jobling as: 'A sophisticated design to grace any occasion, however formal.' The colour is screen printed onto each flat item e.g. plates, and applied as a transfer to the hollow items, e.g. cups. It was produced in a second colourway, green and powder blue for a short period. The design continued into the 1980s, and Jobling produced a set of melamine table mats in matching design.

This design was produced on Space Saver tea and dinner sets, casserole dishes and mixing bowls, but it is also possible to find some of the earlier shapes carrying this design, such as the rounded shape jug and tea-cups. Soup bowls were produced in both rimmed and jockey-cap styles.

The Chelsea pattern in Teal and Black

Chelsea tea set, steak plate and cereal bowl (above). Melamine stand, casserole dishes, mixing bowls and gravy boat with stand (below).

Classics

This was a series of occasional issues produced as limited runs of special patterns. The one that is most often seen is a white design on a grey sprayed ground. A set of snack servers called the Party Bowl Set, with a chrome stand was produced in this pattern, as was a set of the rounded, lipped mixing bowls.

Grey Classics Party Set

This red pattern on a white ground was also produced on Easy Grip casserole dishes.

Large mixing bowl measuring 10" across

Clear Tableware

Jobling first marketed tableware in clear glass only. During the 1930s, they added decoration in the form of engraved flowers, and a cut glass design. The engraving evolved into the Willow Pattern design.

Set of six ramekins with handles number 1482, marked JP.

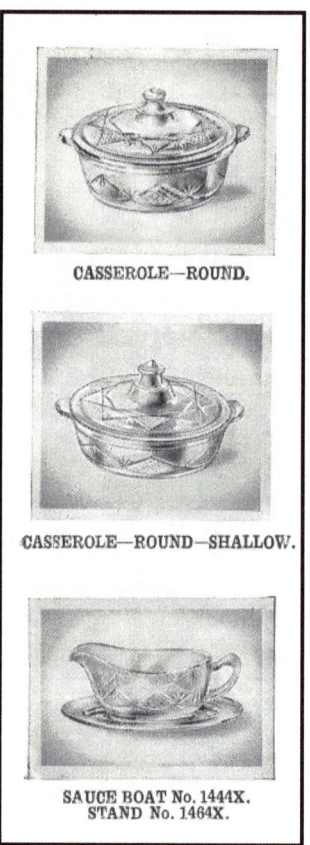

CASSEROLE—ROUND.

CASSEROLE—ROUND—SHALLOW.

SAUCE BOAT No. 1444X.
STAND No. 1464X.

"PYREX" Oven-Table Glassware

Regd. Trade Mark BRAND

ENGRAVED CASSEROLE—CHICKEN
No. 1484 E2 - 3½pt. 8/6
To hold Chicken about 4lbs. in weight.

ENGRAVED SAUCE BOAT AND STAND
No. 1444E Boat - 3/9
No. 1464E Stand - 3/-

ENGRAVED CASSEROLE
—Oval Deep
No. A293 E2 - 8/-
No. A297 E2 - 9/6
No. A294 E2 - 10/6
No. A290 E2 - 16/-

ALL BRITISH MADE.

GLOBE SHAPE TEAPOT.

CASSEROLE—ROUND.

CASSEROLE—OVAL—SHALLOW.

CASSEROLE—SQUARE.
No. A800 E2.

ENGRAVED TEAPOTS—
Globe
No. 12 E - 11/6
No. 14 E - 14/-
No. 16 E - 16/6

ENGRAVED CASSEROLE
—Round
No. A267 E2 - 8/-
No. A268 E2 - 9/6
No. A269 E2 - 10/6
No. A270 E2 - 13/6

ENGRAVED CASSEROLE
—Oval Shallow
No. A283 E2 - 8/-
No. A284 E2 - 9/6
No. A285 E2 - 10/6

ENGRAVED CASSEROLE
—Square
No. A800 E2 - 12/-

ENGRAVED COFFEE POT
No 42 E - 9/3
No. 44 E - 11/6
No. 46 E - 14/3

ENGRAVED FISH OR MEAT PLATTER—Oval
No. 313E
13¾" × 8¾" × 1⅜" 7/3

ENGRAVED CUSTARD CUP
No. 410E 4 ozs. 9d.

Guaranteed against breakage in oven use for Twelve Months from date of purchase

CASSEROLE—CHICKEN.
No. 1484 E2

ENGRAVED SAUCE BOAT AND STAND. Nos. 1444E and 1464E.

CASSEROLE—OVAL—DEEP.

ENGRAVED COFFEE POT.

ENGRAVED FISH OR MEAT PLATTER—OVAL.

ENGRAVED CUSTARD CUP.
No. 410E.

Housewives would have been in no doubt about the many uses of PYREX clear cookware:

- Flavour-saver pie dish – all the nourishment kept captive till the pie is cut! 1 pint 4s 2d, 2 pint 6s.
- Soufflé dish for baking, stewing, serving sweets and savouries – an ideal cake-bake too! 2½ pint 6s.
- Jelly mould – for blancmanges, too – and gelatined meats, eggs, game, 1pint 3s
- General purpose dish has dozens of uses. Cook and serve straight from oven to table, 10s 9d
- Baking dish for the joint and potatoes – or 8lb turkey.

Items marked JAJ (left) and earlier pieces marked JP (below).

Scalloped shells were produced in three sizes, costing 1s, 1s 2d or 1s 10d.

Clover-Leaf

The Clover design was used on a Salad Set produced at the end of the 1950s. This comprised a large salad bowl, with a smaller bowl for dips or dressings balanced ingeniously on a wire stand above the larger bowl. The larger bowl was green with white decoration, and the smaller bowl was green on white. This was linked closely with the Gaiety Range.

Clover Leaf design in white on green and green on white.

Coronet

This, along with Wild Bryony, was the first design to be applied to the Opal base, and was screen-printed. It became available from 1957 in green or red. The spiky pattern epitomised 1950s atomic design, and was printed onto tea and dinner services.

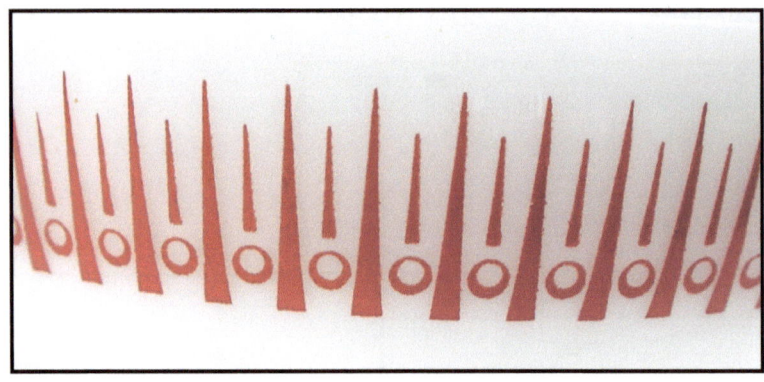

The atomic Coronet design was produced green and red.

Cottage Rose

Cottage Rose is very similar to June Rose, in pale pink instead of red, and with the addition of lily-of-the-valley sprays. Leaves in two shades of green and pale blue add depth to the design. Although these flowers are typical of the 1950s, this design was produced in the 1960s, using the Space Saver shape. It was a widely available design, appearing on tea and dinner services, casserole dishes and mixing bowls.

The design had two variants, to fit on large and small items.

Country Rose on small, eared bowls and on a tea set.

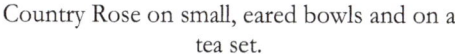

Fiesta

At a time when overseas travel was becoming more accessible to the general public, Spanish, French and Mexican designs proliferated in all areas of British design. Jobling's Fiesta design is just one of these, featuring not only the subject matter of the late 1950s, but also the very trendy line-drawing style. A limited palette of red, yellow, lime green and two shades of blue are used to represent a Mediterranean tabletop, complete with a bottle of Chianti.

This design seems to have appeared at the time Jobling was changing from Easy-Grip to Space Saver shapes, as it appears on items of both shapes.

The Fiesta design was produced on both Space Saver and Easy Grip casserole dishes.

Gaiety

Introduced in 1958, the Gaiety range included Snowflake and Daisy patterns, screen-printed onto casserole dishes. The Snowflake range came in black on white or yellow, and white on blue, black or deep coral, while the white daisies appeared on a pink or yellow ground. The opal body was sprayed, and the snowflake or daisy design was screen printed on top. The design, which showed 'elegance combined with practicability', had been 'especially decorated to blend with the look of any table and the furnishings of any room'.

Described by Jobling as 'made in pearly white opal glass, decorated with a black snowflake motif and further embellished by a gold rim', the dinner service, brought out in 1959, was seen as a high spot in PYREX glass merchandising history. Marketed as 'gay and gifty', it was hoped that the new range would 'hallmark the company as style leaders of the oven-glass market', and was aimed at the gift market, for Christmas, weddings etc.

The Gooseberry pattern was available on a Space Saver casserole set in deep coral/white or green/white. Jobling also produced a Wild Rose design as part of this range, which was a band of roses in gold on an ivory ground.

Wild Rose design

The Gaiety Snowflake 21-piece tea service for six persons comprised: 6 side plates, 6 cups/saucers, 1 bread plate, 1 milk jug, 1 sugar bowl, and was marketed alongside the Weardale range. Pieces can be found in both Space Saver and Easy-Grip shapes.

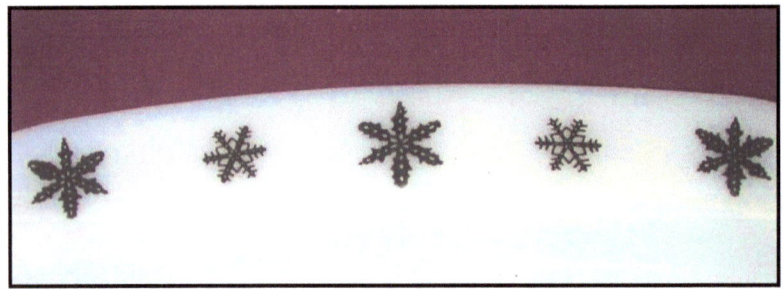

The Gaiety design

In 1959, a set of four mixing bowls would be 45s. A divided vegetable dish (blue, black, pink or yellow) with stand was 35s. A Gaiety dinner service would cost you £6.6.0 and by 1965 still cost under £7.

Part of a recipe leaflet produced in 1962 to promote the Gaiety and Weardale ranges. This leaflet plays on the growing trend for foreign travel, and the widening global knowledge brought about by the increased availability of television sets, by showing recipes from other countries.

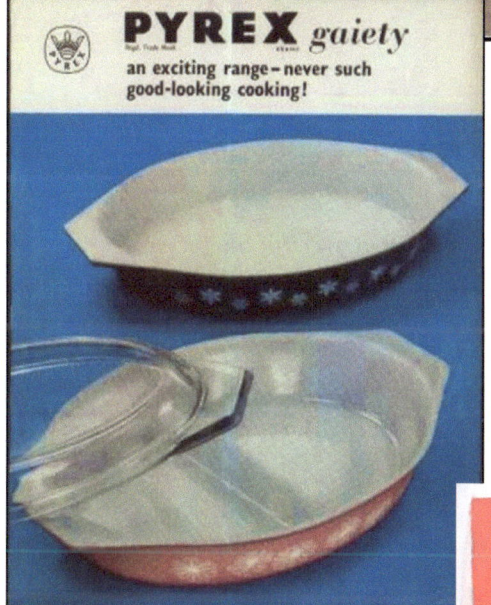

Advert for vegetable serving dishes (left) and one of the various boxes that were produced for Gaiety cookware (below).

Two-page advert that ran in 1965, with the slogan 'Get acquainted' followed by 'Now meet the family'.

Gooseberry

Introduced in 1959, this design was part of the Gaiety range and was seen on mixing bowls and casserole dishes only. These items are all screen-printed with a design showing gooseberries on the bush. Bowls came in a choice of white on deep coral, or deep coral on white, blue/white and white/blue, and white on yellow. It was later produced in white/pink and pink/white and black on yellow.

Gooseberry design in black on a white ground

Yellow Gooseberry mixing bowl and green casserole dish.

Gooseberry set in turquoise and white

Green Line

At the very end of the 1930s, Green Line was one of Jobling's first forays into the wonderful world of colour. It featured two fine concentric lines in an olive shade, and was applied using a turntable.

This sauce boat is marked with the JP logo. The outside is sprayed with pale green enamel, and the darker green line is hand-painted onto the inside of the dish.

Harvest

Once again, the mood of the times had an influence on design, and Harvest shows the impact of foreign travel on the UK. This design shows English vegetables portrayed in vibrant colours, very reminiscent of Spanish style. The bright red carrots could easily be mistaken for peppers. As the subject matter is more suitable for dinners or suppers than afternoon tea, the design appeared on casserole dishes, mixing bowls and dinner services, but not on tea sets. It appears on the straight lines of the Space Saver range as well as the more rounded Easy Grip shape.

Hostess Set

This was seen as a single item, not a set, and comprised four coloured bowls (two yellow, two red) on a silver-coloured serving stand. A very similar item had been marketed earlier, with the Classics design, under the name Party Bowl Set.

Hostess Set showing it's gold-coloured stand and white plastic handle.

Hunting Scene

Hunting Scene was produced as part of the Space Saver range on a wide range of items. It is a complex design, using many layered colours, and shows two huntsmen accompanied by their hounds. Tea sets, dinner services, casseroles and mixing bowls all carried the design, and they were supported by mini-trays and ash-trays, which could be used as tiny serving dishes, change trays or spoon rests.

The tea set of Hunting Scene was marketed in association with the tea firm Rington's under the name Tally-Ho. Customers of Rington's tea could collect tokens, which were then exchanged for PYREX items, enabling them to build up a whole tea set. It was introduced in the 1960s, and was a transfer applied to white Opalware. Although hunting it is not now considered politically correct, the design was very popular and continues to remind us of our social history.

'Tally-Ho' tea set number 333-146, available to customers for 25/- on purchase of half a pound of Red Label tea.

This punch bowl was warmed by a candle in the stand, and appeared in an advert in 1962 aimed at the younger generation. This was a break-through in advertising initiatives, as Jobling advertising had previously been aimed at the married woman.

Hunting Scene ash tray with smoked glass (below)

Indiana

A modern design with a country feel, produced on casserole dishes.

June Rose

June Rose featured an open rose and a rose bud in Blossom Red and Foliage Green. The design was altered to fit the smaller pieces, so tea cups, for instance, featured a single rose-bud instead of a spray. First introduced in September of 1964, it was produced by the screen-printed transfer method, which gives a heavy enamel deposit with a glossy finish. There were initially twenty-five items in the range, and it was chosen from a list of eight motifs as 'a modern expression of the traditional'.

As with Chelsea, this design was predominantly produced as a Space Saver set, but was also produced on some Easy-Grip items. This is one of the ranges that feature the jockey-cap bowl.

The June Rose design was altered to fit onto smaller items by removing the full-blown rose, to leave only the bud and a small spray of leaves.

Mixing bowl and large soufflé dish (above), casserole set (right) showing how the design is enlarged to fit larger pieces, and one of the later style boxes (below).

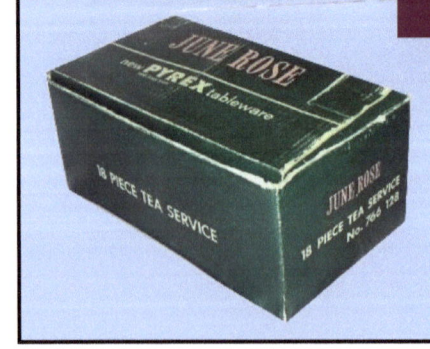

Kent Orchard

Kent Orchard features fruit from the Garden of England, nestling between twigs and leaves. The apple, pear, plums, damsons and cherries are portrayed realistically, as opposed to the stylized Harvest design. This design was produced on Space Saver casserole dishes only.

The Kent Orchard design on round and oval Space Saver casserole dishes.

Kitchenware

The Easy-grip range, which was introduced at the beginning of the 1950s, included half pint and 1pt measuring jugs, mixing bowls, a 15" rolling pin, oval and round casseroles, non-topple pudding basins, plates, a rectangular general purpose dish, sauceboats, jelly mould, scalloped shells, soufflé dish, flavour-saver pie dish, and a baster, which retailed at 6/10.

The baster was a popular item, and was even advertised as 'a wonderful bridge or party gift', and was used to separate cream from milk, or grease from gravy as well as basting the Sunday joint.

The 'Practical Pie Funnel' (left) and the measuring bowl with pouring spout (below).

A set of mixing bowls with a clean white opal inside, and s bright sprayed outside. These bowls are an unusual departure from the Jobling trademark pastel colours.

An advert for Colourware items, including Easy-Grip pudding basins with non-topple design – the 1 pint bowl was 2s, the 1½ pint was 2s 9d and the 2½ pint was 3s 9d.

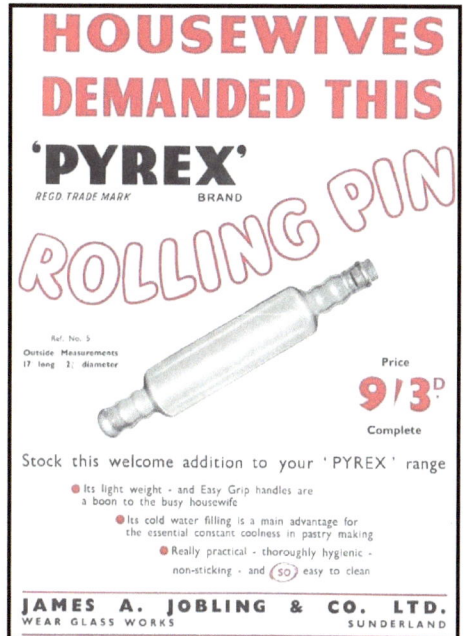

The first rolling pin to be added to the PYREX range had one cork stopper only and measured 17" long. This would have cost the housewife 9s 3d.

The main selling points were the fact that you could fill it with cold water to maintain 'essential constant coolness in pastry making' and the fact this it was 'thoroughly hygienic' because it was so easy to clean.

A PYREX rolling pin with its original box

The 15" rolling pin was introduced with the Easy-grip range gand had two corks with red stoppers. It retailed for 8s.

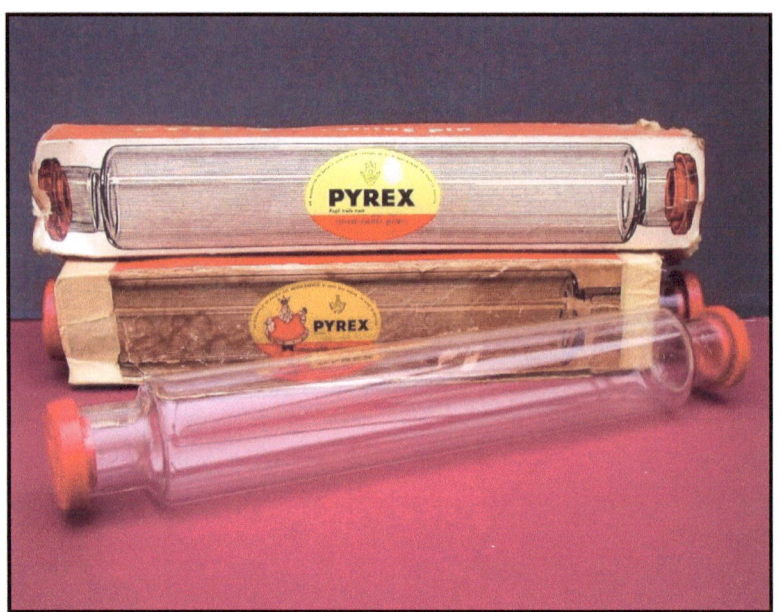

The later design rolling pin with end caps in claret plastic. Both boxes are badly damaged, but are included to show both types of red and yellow logo.

The symbol used on the end caps of the rolling pin had a condensed version of the letters JAJ, with the letters interlocked.

'Mix with it – cocoa, patent beverages, baby foods, custards – almost all powders and liquids can be mixed quickly and smoothly with'

'Whisk with it – eggs, egg whites, cream, hot chocolate – everything to a fine froth'

'Blend with it – sweet and savoury sauces, icing mixtures, finely chopped herb sauces – and even other creams and sauces using butter (you can safely stand your PYREX mixer in hot water of course) ... all blend, easily, quickly'

600cc or 1 pt capacity mixer

The PYREX mixer was sold in conjunction with Horlicks, and it is often known as 'the Horlicks mixer'.

Jelly moulds promised 'perfect jellies, blancmanges, gelatine savouries'. The 1pt size, number 276, cost 2/6.

A set of Stack n Store Jars (right) with clip-on lids, put onto the market in 1973 These were also available with cream lids, and came with a selection of stick-on labels for the housewife to use.

The kitchen utensils set (below) was only produced for a few years before being withdrawn. It is unusual to find a set still in its original box.

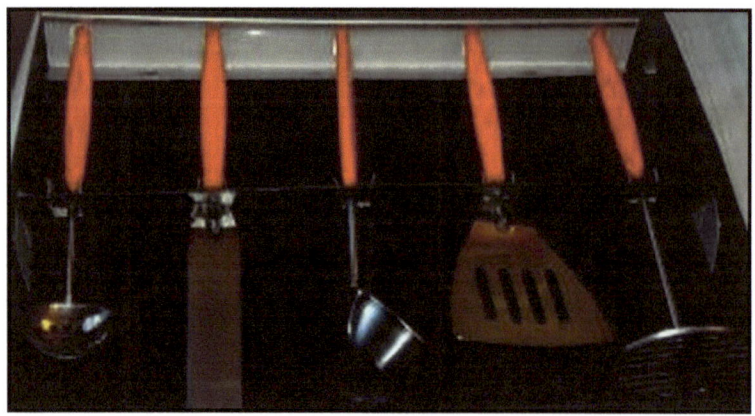

'Pyrex' Clear Kitchenware Complete Range

177. 2½ pt mix-n-measure bowl

170. (1 pt), 171. (1½ pt) 172. (2 pt) pudding basin

195. 1½ pt oblong pie dish

251. 8½" pie plate

198. 2 pt flavour saver pie dish

270. 1¾ pt flan dish

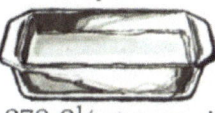
278. 2½ pt general purpose dish

183. 3½ pt mixing bowl
184. 5 pt mixing bowl

260. ½ pt measuring jug
261. 1 pt measuring jug

276. 1 pt jelly mould

271. Square roaster

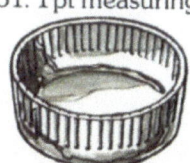
279. 1¾ pt souffle dish
272. 2½ pt souffle dish

490044 1 litre stack-n-store jars (pair)

190. (¾ pt), 191. (1¼ pt)
192. (2 pt) oval pie dish

430. Rolling pin

491040/1. 2 litre stack-n-store jar (light or dark brown lid).

Details of the Space Saver range of kitchenware.

Lobster

What a fabulous design! No holding back here – this is bright, bold and beautiful. Lobster was printed in hot shades of orange and lime green, tempered by cool blues, onto Easy-Grip casserole dishes. The design was reduced in size to fit on to the smaller items, rather than being altered by having some elements removed.

Lobster design

Market Garden

The Market Garden design features a radish and a cauliflower, amongst other vegetables. It was advertised as 'A gay variety of garden produce to cheer up the dining table and give everyone a healthy appetite.' This design was renamed for export, and marketed as Tuscany (see below). There is also another very similar design with a cob of sweetcorn featuring prominently. This design was only produced on Space Saver casserole dishes, and on tableware, although this is rarely seen nowadays. There were three sizes of the regular casserole shape, three sizes of the deep shape, and a rectangular dish, too, as well as the collectable individual casserole dish. The range was marketed with the help of a cartoon market gardener, complete with spats and a straw in his mouth.

The market gardener designed to promote the Market Garden design.

Market Garden design on Space Saver casseroles.

Tuscany

As our home-grown Harvest has an international brother in the Tropical Fruit pattern, so the Market Garden design of British food has a Tuscan relative – this time, a twin! Tuscany a popular design, and became one of Jobling's best-sellers.

Matchmaker

This abstract set shows stripes of Sky Blue and Sage Green in alternating blocks, and initially had twenty-five pieces in the range. Introduced in September 1964, it was also produced in the less well-known red/orange colourway. It is a screen-printed pattern, and was intended to complement the June Rose design, which was launched in the same month. This design was seen as 'an abstract for the individualist', while June Rose catered for more traditional tastes.

Printed onto the Space Saver shape opalware, this design appears on a large range of items, including tea sets, dinner services, mixing bowls and casserole dishes. The soup bowls show the jockey-cap elliptical handle.

Blue/green colourway (above) and red/yellow (below)

Poppies and Sunflowers

Poppies and Sunflowers were two of the last designs brought out by Jobling, showing vibrantly coloured flowers. Very much a symbol of the early 1970s, when both flowers were available on crockery, furnishings and clothing, these designs once again show Jobling's ability to change with fashion, and reflect the mood of the era. Being later designs, they were produced on Space Saver shapes, and on dinner services, mixing bowls and casserole dishes. There was a Sunflowers tea set, but not a Poppies one.

The popular Sunflowers design (above) and Poppies (below)

Pyrex Royal

This range comprised a White Hawthorn design on a lusciously deep green, blue or red ground, and also the Wildfowl design (see below). Both designs have a gold rim. It also appears on matching mixing bowls in Olive Green on white, or red on white.

Despite being a very traditional design, reminiscent of fine china tableware, this has the modern lines of the Space Saver Range. It was produced on casserole dishes, mixing bowls and dinner services only.

The Hawthorn design in white on green (left) and Olive Green on white (below)

Red Hawthorn on a white ground.

The Red, Green and Blue of PYREX Royal. Being coated with enamel colour, these items tended to scratch easily and it is hard to find an unmarked set.

Silver Servers

PYREX glass was marketed in a variety of silver-coloured holders, to make the clear glass more attractive to the housewife. Even the ramekins had their own little holders! Tumblers came with chromium-plated holders. An alternative to these holders was a chromium-plated frame, to protect your table from the heat.

Oval Streamline Casserole dish with an EPNS holder. The lid is numbered S-293-C, and the base S-193-B. It is interesting to note that it also has 'Registration Applied For' embossed on the lid.

Frames continued to be produced to protect the table, in simplified form, throughout the Jobling reign, with white or black plastic handles. In the 1970s they were improved with the addition of teak handles.

This deep oval pie dish has a pewter holder. The lid is missing, but the number on the base is A-197-B. The base is marked with the JP logo.

'Pride of England' casserole dish stamped 53-4 on the lid. The base has the JP logo on it. This dish has an aluminium holder with bakelite handles and base. The price on the box is 27/6.

Early 1.5pt round casserole dish in EPNS stand. The lid is marked 267C, and the stand is hallmarked.

Oval casserole dish in a highly polished EPNS holder. The lid is marked A 283 OR 297-C, and the base is marked A-197-B. This design has only three feet, two shown at the front, and one at the back

Tea and Coffee Sets

Tea and coffee sets have always featured prominently in the PYREX range, from the early days, when they were both produced in clear glass. The straining/filtering parts of the tea and coffee pots could be bought separately. As early as 1936, PYREX glass was advertising tumblers with Bakelite handles for the Christmas market. These were presented in silver foil gift boxes.

The back of a 1920s PYREX cookery book designed to show the full range of cookware.

Half-pint tumblers with bakelite holders only 3/-, or 5/8 with holder.

Tall Tumblers were introduced in 1956 in a red or yellow plastic holder, to be used with the holder for hot drinks, and without for cold. Customers were encouraged to use the PYREX serving bowl with candle warmer stand (see Hunting Scene) to serve hot punch.

The blown glass 'Instant Coffee Jug' was brought onto the market in 1958, and with it's gold metallic band and black plastic handle/lid, it conformed with the 1950s 'atomic' design trend. This item came with a wire stand, which held a tea-light candle to keep the coffee warm at table. It was available in two sizes, costing 27s or 32s 6d.

Gold vine decoration was introduced in 1959, on a matching decanter, to cater for the newly-travelled leisure classes, who brought back from their holidays a taste for chianti and liebfraumilch.

Over the next few years, a coffee maker (with spirit heater), lidded jug and sugar basin were added to the range. The use of a single stand soon extended, when Jobling brought out the Coffee and Tea Set with its own serving stand.

In the mid-sixties, the Drinkmasters range was introduced, with coloured Drinkups, and a new plastic tray to replace the previously manufactured metallic one. The style of the Drinkup plastic holder was refined at the end of the decade, with a change to the shape of the handle. Drinkups came in green, yellow, red, orange, grey, maroon, or in mixed sets.

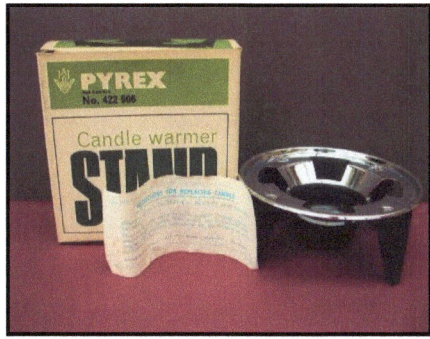

This candle warmer stand came with a Price's candle and full instructions. It was number 422-906.

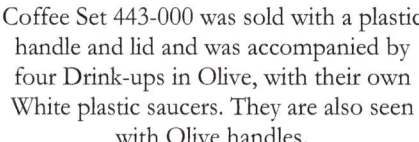

Coffee Set 443-000 was sold with a plastic handle and lid and was accompanied by four Drink-ups in Olive, with their own White plastic saucers. They are also seen with Olive handles.

Juggler coffee jugs were introduced in 1973, making the most of the new craze for coloured plastics, and in the 1970s a filter coffee jug (the Coffee Fresh Set), and then an instant coffee were added to the range.

The Juggler jug was available in brown or bright orange.

Silver Clover Leaf Tea and Coffee Set with six cup coffee and tea jug, two cup jug and sugar bowl with prices Calorette candle. Old number 29, new number 440 013.

The Clover Leaf design came in both gold and silver, and was introduced in 1962.

Jug with gold clover leaf design for use with 'instant tea, coffee, milk, cream, custard. This four-cup jug is numbered 32.

Instant Coffee Jug number 21 (right) and Four Drinkups numbered 403-015 (below).

Electric Warming Plate 300 509 for use with PYREX Coffee and Tea jugs (right).

Tempo

Tempo shows bold flowers in blue, green, brown and orange, repeated in a strip pattern. This design is described by Jobling as: 'A graceful reminder of another age to add romance to the meal table'. It seems that it was intended to look like an Art Nouveau design, but it rather epitomises the psychedelic, floral art of the early 1970s, when it was marketed.

Tempo was part of the Space Saver range of items, and is one of the designs that were simply enlarged to fit onto different sized dishes. It featured on tea and dinner services, casseroles and mixing bowls, and has become one of the most collectable of the Jobling designs.

Tempo design tea cup and saucer in the Space Saver style

Toledo

This is a 1970s design, showing the brilliant oranges and browns that were the colours of the decade. Stylized flowers and starbursts bring a bit of funky psychedelia to the humdrum world of cooking. This design was produced on Space Saver casserole dishes and mixing bowls.

1970s Circles design (above) shown below on an Easy Grip casserole

Tropical

This design is very similar to Harvest, in that it has the same design style, and features fronds of fennel in the background. However, Tropical seems to be an international counterpart to the domestic Harvest bowl, with a large pineapple prominently in the middle of more English onions, carrots and peas. It was available on Space Saver casserole dishes only.

A lovely example of a new Space Saver casserole dish in the Tropical design

Weardale

Items in the Weardale range were colour sprayed onto an opal base, and had gold rims. Introduced at the same time as the Gaiety range, at the end of the 1950s, Weardale was available in Deep Coral, Duck Egg Blue or Spring Yellow. It has the beautiful curves of the Easy-Grip range, and was available on tea and dinner services and on casserole dishes.

Weardale casserole dishes in Spring Yellow and Deep Coral (top) and a Duck Egg Blue tea-set (below).

Wheatsheaf

Wheatsheaf in red, blue or Olive Green appeared on opal dinner sets, including this divided snack server. This item was also sold with a holder, and could be used for cold snacks as well. Wheatsheaf was not widely produced, but it is possible to find casserole dishes with the design.

Wheatsheaf in green, blue and red

Wild Bryony

In 1957, this design, along with Coronet, was the first design to be offered on domestic tableware, and was screen-printed. It was produced in Charcoal, which was a pleasing contrast to the pearly whiteness of the opal base.

Wild Bryony tea cup and saucer. The edge of a tea plate shows in the bottom left of the pictures.

Wildfowl

Introduced in the 1960s, this design features mallard ducks settling onto the banks of a stream, or flying through clear blue skies, and is part of the PYREX Royal range. It is printed onto a transfer, before being added to the Space Saver opal base. Jobling produced many different items in the Wildfowl pattern, and it is possible to find odd items, such as mini-trays as well as tea sets, dinner services, casseroles and mixing bowls.

One of the three designs in the Wild Fowl range.

Willow Pattern

Willow Pattern engraved onto a clear plate

This was one of the very first designs, produced in the early thirties. The first willow pattern design was press-moulded, to give the impression of a design engraved into the surface. It was then produced by using a layer of blue ink, which rested in the grooves and finally, at the end of the 1930s, a transfer design was brought out. This design was available on both dinner services and casserole dishes.

Other Designs

Jobling produced hundreds of designs, some which made it into full production, and some which never did. Many of them can be firmly linked to the decade in which they originated, such as the Kitchen Shelf design.

Greek Key

A grey continuous edging design, which appeared on tableware only.

Kitchen Shelf

A fabulously 1950s design

Blue daisies

A typical 1970s design.

White printed design

White art nouveau swirls highlighted with tiny dots, printed onto a clear base.

Homestead

This design was brought out during the 1970s, when the fashion was for homespun materials. The soft beige blended well with the natural materials being used in home decoration.

Autumn Harvest

zThis design was not widely available, but has found fame between the pages of Margueritte Patten's Cookery Book. It shows a spray of autumn countryside fruits and leaves, and is probably a transfer design.

Rosehip

The Rosehip design is once again in realistic style, and seems to be the country cousin of June Rose, who seems rather brash in contrast to this delicately drawn study.

Fuchsia

Monochrome design of fuschia flowers reminiscent of a watercolour study.

Mystery design

Unknown abstract band in Air Force Blue.

Apple Blossom

A sweet design, with a Japanese feel to it. Perhaps it is cherry blossom. This is marked JAJ, but was produced very late in the company's history.

In 1973 the company was taken over by Corning. Designs produced after this time include Rocco, Sienna, Harvest Spray, Fireside, Rustic, Vine, the Brasilia range, Butterflies and Songbird, which still bear the JAJ imprint. After 1975 the name of the company was changed to Corning Ltd.

Marks and Labels

The first PYREX glassware, manufactured in the 1920s, was made when the firm was still run by Ernest Jobling Purser and the mark on the bottom of each piece was the JP logo.

Ernest Jobling Purser retired in 1949, and the company was taken over by Pilkington Brothers, who passed it on to Thomas Tilling. By 1953, the company was looking for a new logo, and settled on a crown over the word PYREX.

Later, the letters JAJ, for James A. Jobling, were added to the logo. This continued until the take-over by Corning, when the letters were discontinued.

Flameware had its own mark when it was introduced in 1952.

The PYREX King was introduced in 1956, wearing the PYREX crown. In one campaign, he did forsake his crown, in favour of boxing gloves, to show the company was coming out fighting. He was first used on items being sent overseas, to remind customers of their British origin, but was soon put on items for the home market too, to let the housewife know she was buying British.

There are a variety of logos to source and collect, and they are mirrored by the number of guarantee labels and box designs. Originally in plain brown cardboard, with labels attached, the box designs improved in design as technology advanced.

At the time of its greatest popularity, PYREX from Jobling was packaged in distinctive red and yellow boxes, and guarantee labels were produced to match.

The red and yellow box colours were replaced in later years by blue, green and orange boxes, which were themselves eventually superseded by a wide range of colours, as each design acquired its own box design.

Every item of PYREX glass produced from the 1950s onwards was sold with its own sticker attached and each box had its own guarantee, ranging from six months in the early years, through one year and two years, to the '2001' range which was produced in the 1970s and guaranteed until the year 2001.

Two-year guarantee label (left) and one of the stickers that appeared on each item of PYREX to guarantee its provenance (right).

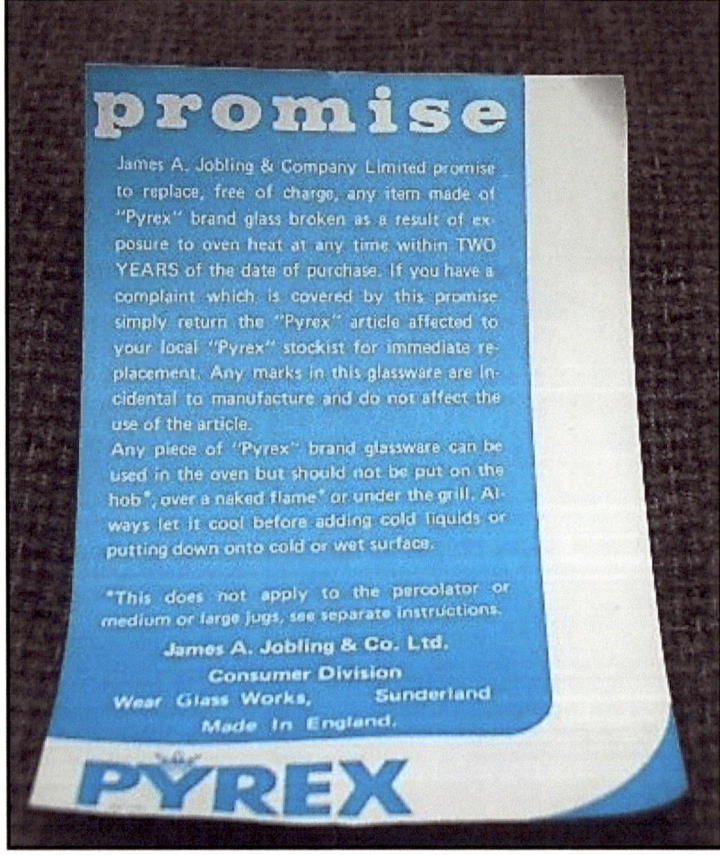

One of the very first guarantees (top) stamped by the retailed, and a much later two-year guarantee leaflet (below).

JAJ Collectables

There are two types of collectables associated with the JAJ factory's production of PYREX glass. Firstly, the multitude of paper ephemera that always accompanies production of this sort: flyers, posters, magazine adverts, photos and house magazines. Secondly, there is the diverse range of items associated with a large, traditionally run company: company ties, beer glasses, mugs, photographs, motoring club badges, etc. Company ties were available from the Personnel Dept at Jobling for 10/6 each, which was cost price, and had the PYREX crest on them in gold, against a claret background.

PYREX regularly produced cookery books, and these were tested in the PYREX kitchen. The PYREX Modern Cookery Book (left) was available 'free of cost', and coupons appeared in many women's magazines during the early 1930s. It first appeared in 1927, and has a foreword written by the Principal of The National School of Cookery, E. Gladys Clarke.

The PYREX Family enjoy a meal served from Autumn Glory cookware on to matching plates in Spring 1971 (left).

The 1950s cookbook on the right shows a variety of recipes using Streamline cookware.

The 1962 leaflet (left) was produced to advertise the new Gaiety range of cookware, and encourages the housewife to 'be adventurous and gain full marks as a hostess of vision!' Recipes include moussaka, beef stroganoff and chilli con carne.

A laminated set of recipe cards (above) produced to advertise the new Space Saver shapes introduced in the 1970s.

The PYREX Book of Regional Cookery was published in 1977.

The marketing department at the Jobling works also recognised the role played by the shop assistants and store owners who had direct contact with the customer. They produced advertising material aimed directly at these people. One of their campaigns in the mid-1950s to encourage

further sales from their outlets was the Spring Profit Building Plan and In-Store Flower Promotion. This ran from 1st March until 17th April, and promised that an eye-catching display would add consumer appeal and lead to greater sales.

The PYREX Home Centre at the Jobling factory was set up to train sales staff in the uses of PYREX ware. Sales assistants from firms throughout the country were offered a free one-week residential course, which covered a tour of the factory and a series of lectures covering glass design, display, presentation and salesmanship.

4oz Feeding Bottle numbered 310-000 and a bottle packaged in a later design box.

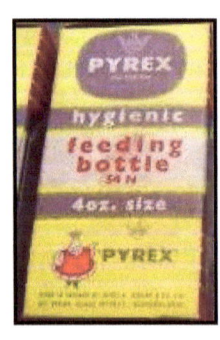

Illustrated price lists for the retailer from the 1930s (left) and the 1940s (below).

Jobling worked with other companies to promote PYREX items, such as Maws baby bottles and Horlicks hot drinks. These items are sought after by collectors of other brand names as well as those collecting JAJ ware.

Jobling has always had a strong tradition of promoting PYREX, and adverts regularly appeared in women's magazines. At the beginning of the sixties, Jobling boasted that their advertising would reach one in every two women. The advert on the right from the 1950s is directed at brides-to-be compiling their wedding lists.

A Christmas advert from the 1960s showing a white Gaiety dinner set and Gaiety cookware alongside Colourware bowls and blown glass coffee jugs.

Advert for Colourware items. Notice that this advert promotes the red items that were only produced for a short time.

Magazine advert from Christmas 1955 showing clear and coloured PYREX.

PYREX glass was such a desirable item that it even appeared as one of the free gifts offered to new subscribers to The Foyles Book Clubs. This pastel-coloured baking set is especially sought-after as a modern collectable. The enamel is

 sprayed on to an opal body. Advertised as 'without a doubt, ... one of the most outstanding gifts which even The Book Clubs have offered!'

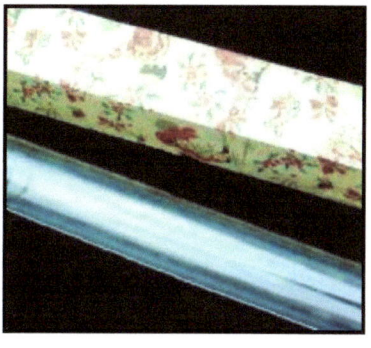

Jobling liked to grasp any advertising opportunity they could, and as Christmas approached, many of their items were available in special packaging.

Tally-Ho and rolling pin Christmas boxes.

Jobling produced a quarterly company magazine called Mixed Batch, which gave more than letters from management, details of awards for innovative ideas, and information on new developments. The magazine included photographs of Sports Days, the crowning of The Glass Queen, the employees' family Christmas lunch, and featured employee details. The whole magazine had a light-hearted tone, and was very much produced by the employees for the employees.

Copies of the Mixed Batch house magazine (above) showing various cover designs, and a PYREX tea towel with Autumn Glory design (right).

Commemorative Ware

Jobling produced numerous pieces for other companies featuring their logos, from ashtrays to whole dinner sets. Two of the most important links were with Horlicks and Maws, for which they made mixers and feeding bottles, respectively. They also produced commemorative-ware for events, such as the Coronation in 1953

In 1966, some of the World Cup matches were held at Roker Park, home of Sunderland Football Club, and Jobling produced a set of six PYREX tumblers decorated with views of landmarks in Sunderland.

Items produced for the Queen's Coronation in 1953 (above) and for her Silver Jubilee in 1977 (right).

A Coronation beer tankard was produced in 1953, but was made in Flint Glass, not PYREX. However, it was sold alongside PYREX, and attracted the same discounts for buyers.

In 1973, Sunderland Football Club won the F.A. Cup, and Jobling's was quick to celebrate with a souvenir ash tray.

Working at the Jobling Factory

The Jobling's Plant was the second largest employer in the area and whole families enjoyed the privileges this brought. The departments were close-knit communities, with the normal jealousies and rivalries that arose from this kind of working relationship. Clubs and societies welcomed a mix of members, while events such as sports day defined loyalty to departments.

Of course, life at the factory should not be viewed through rose-tinted spectacles. Pilfering at the plant was reported in the Sunderland Echo on March 23rd 1942. A young woman from Pennywell was accused of stealing six PYREX plates from James A. Jobling Ltd. Chief Inspector Middlemist told the court it was estimated that 10% of the factory's produce was being stolen.

A Drama Group was started in 1953 and produced its first play in October, at The Royalty Theatre. This same year saw the launch of the Sailing Club.

Departments included: Conveyers, Glassmakers, Laboratories & Drawing, Sales, Transport, General Office, Building and Maintenance, Engineering, Electricians, Advertising, Work Study, Costs, Purchasing, Glass Technology, Production Control, Commissionaires, Pressware, Home Centre, Research, Tubing, Stores, Order/Invoice, SA, Decorating, Personnel, Flint, Apparatus, and Wages. Members of these departments appeared regularly in the Mixed Batch magazine, with details of recent departmental activities. The magazine also included details of weddings, retirements and obituaries, departmental gossip, a regular photographic competition and pages of interest to ladies, such as recipes and fashion tips.

The efficiency of the packing and transport system was much appreciated by the retailers. Graham Hall recalls:

> "Let me start back in 1967. I left school and joined a small hardware wholesaler, which supplied shops in Derbyshire and neighbouring counties. They actually stocked PYREX glass in a big way, all of the clearware, and at the time, the three current designs June Rose, Matchmaker and Gaiety. A delivery from Jobling was a major nightmare, this company was in a residential area, not a lot of space for parking the huge articulated lorries that delivered PYREX glass, so a quieter nearby street had to be found to transfer some 700/800 cartons, from the artic that reversed up to the rear of a transit sized van, so that this could be reversed to the bottom of the yard in some ramshackle buildings where it was stored. It was fine when PYREX ware was actually delivered by the company themselves, naturally everything was loaded in order which made the transfer easy. Occasionally it was delivered by public carrier, which was an absolute nightmare."

Jobling ran a successful Staff Suggestion Scheme, whereby employees were rewarded with cash payments for any ideas taken up by the company. These ideas ranged from safety considerations to design proposals, and although initially only open to salaried staff, in 1955 the scheme was extended to include weekly paid staff, and to increase the initial award from £6 to £12. Ideas had to be for something not related to the employee's normal work. In the Coronation year, two suggestions that were taken up were for a coronation tumbler, and for a 'Royal Ermine' sugar bowl.

The club badge of the Motoring Section of the Social Club.

In 1952, Jobling set up a Civil Defence Force, and offered employees a course covering Civil Defence Organisation, Fire Fighting, Chemical Warfare, High Explosives, Protective Measures, Atomic Bombs etc.

Many aspects of the glass industry carried serious Health and Safety issues and first aid was often needed. Where most companies had a First Aid room, Jobling had an Ambulance Room staffed by uniformed nurses.

Jobling had Bowling, Cricket, Badminton, Swimming, Tennis and Football clubs. Sports Day was held at The Grange, Hylton, and featured traditional running and relay races alongside the Ladies Potato Race, Tug-o-War, 3-legged Race, Ladies Endurance Skipping and Children's Races. The Grange had a full range of facilities, including tennis courts, swings, tea-rooms and a family room with a television set.

1953. The Engineering Team win the Tug-o-War at the annual Sports Day

Where coal-mining communities elected an annual Coal Queen, Jobling elected a Glass Queen and princesses. In 1953, twenty-six girls competed for the title of Wear Glass Queen although by 1956 this figure had risen to forty-seven. Miss Doreen Watson, a 19-year-old shorthand typist was the winner of the 1956/7 title. That night, in 1956, the party went on until 1am, as the girls danced with their proud families. The evening included a dance and was always a sell-out event. In 1957 800 people attended.

The 1956/7 Queen and her Attendants

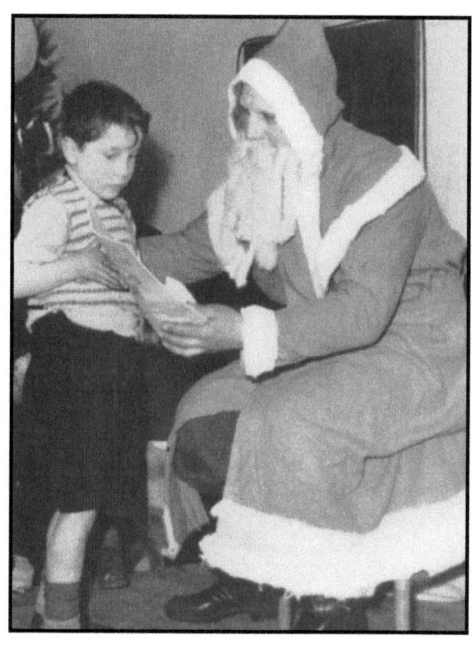

An Annual Company Dinner was put on for the male employees with three or more years' service. 1953 saw 700 attendees, which rose to 1,000 by 1957. Past employees were also invited back to these dinners as Pensioners. Judging from cartoons of the event and oblique references in the Mixed Batch magazine, these were thoroughly enjoyed by everyone and the obligatory round of speeches never overshadowed people's enjoyment of the plentiful food and drink at hand.

One annual event that was popular with the younger members of the employees' families was the Christmas Party. Party hats, party food, a tree and Father Christmas – in the days before commercial overload it must have been a terrific afternoon for the youngsters.

Each child had tea and was given a gift, fruit and sweets. The younger children watched Punch & Judy and a ventriloquist act, while the older ones were entertained by a film show. By 1958, the workforce was so large, and the parties so popular, that they had to be split into two, with 300 children attending each one.

The Mixed Batch reports that the Ladies Social Evening in 1952 had 250 attendees, who had to leave in time to catch the late trams and buses home.

One man who received national recognition for his work at Jobling was Charles Hunter. In 1963 he received the B.E.M., and appeared in the Sunderland Echo.

Mr Hunter (left) designed and made the stands upon which PYREX glass was displayed at fairs and exhibitions, and his children, Dorothy and Raymond (below), often helped their mother in the PYREX kitchen, where recipes were tested.

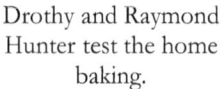

Drothy and Raymond Hunter test the home baking.

Dorothy and Raymond in the kitchen.

Dorothy recalls those days fondly, remarking that they were allowed to help with every aspect of the cooking, even taking the hot food out of the oven. "Safety didn't seem to be so much of an issue as it is nowadays!" she laughs.

The history of the Jobling factory is peppered with stories like this. The town of Sunderland saw generations of workers pass through the factory gates and come out again with tales to tell.

Cyril Easton started at the factory in 1949 and worked there for 35 years. If you are lucky, you can still catch him at a WI or Mothers Union meeting talking about the history of glassmaking in the area and his days at Jobling. This book gives the bare bones of the history of British PYREX, but stories from people like Cyril breathe life into it.

PYREX glassware forms part of our social history. Remember it, record it, and be proud!

Durham Constabulary PYREX ash tray or change tray

Appendix

CODE	DESCRIPTION	SIZE
N0/N1/N2/N2A/N3	Coffee bowl to fit any standard coffee making machine	
N0/N1/N2/N2A/N3	Coffee funnels to fit any standard coffee making machine	
1	Tumbler, plain	
2	Tumbler, flanged top, packed in cartons of 6	½ pint
3	Tumbler with handle, plain	
4	Tumbler with handle, flanged	
5	Rolling pin with one cork stopper	
6	Tumbler with chromium plated holder packed in cartons of 6. Holders packed separately	½ pint
8	Tumbler in Bakelite holder	½ pint
?	Silver plated metal frame tumbler holder	
9	Pie cup supplied in cartons of 6	
10	Measuring cup (this is actually a jug shape)	10oz
11	Teapot, globe shape	1 cup
12	Teapot, globe shape	2 cups
12 E	Teapot, engraved with flowers	
14	Teapot, globe shape	4 cups

14 E	Teapot, engraved with flowers	
16	Teapot, globe shape	6 cups
16 E	Teapot, engraved with flowers	
18, later 401	Clear glass tumbler in plastic holder	½ pint
19 later 431 000	Mixer	
20, later 261	Measuring jug	1pt
21, later 260	Measuring jug	½ pint
21	Instant coffee jug on brass plated candle warmer stand	2pint
22	Teapot, low shape	2 cups
24	Teapot, low shape	4 cups
25, later 433	Decanter with vine decoration	Height 9.5"
26	Teapot, low shape	6 cups
27, later 420	Coffee maker with stand and spirit heater	1½ pint
32	Coffee pot/ tea pot, tall shape	2 cups
34	Coffee pot/ tea pot, tall shape	4 cups
36	Coffee pot/ tea pot, tall shape	6 cups
42	Coffee pot	
42 E	Coffee pot engraved with flowers	
44	Coffee pot	4 cups
44 E	Coffee pot, engraved with flowers	
46	Coffee pot	6 cups

46 E	Coffee pot, engraved with flowers	
48W	Feeding bottle, wide mouth	8oz
53	Beer mug	
58N	Single-ended nursing bottle	8oz
60	Measuring jug	1½ pint
68NR	Feeding bottle	8oz
100	Space Saver Individual casserole, clear	8oz
TS101	Flameware skillet	
102	Space Saver clear, round casserole	1pint
108	Space Saver clear round casserole	2pint
110	Covered entrée dish, reversible - cover	10 5/8" x 8" x 2 7/8"
110D	Avon pattern entrée dish	
110W	Entrée dish with Willow Pattern design	
B110W	Entrée dish in blue Willow Pattern	
112/A112	Round casserole (shallow) OR entrée dish, round, covered	1½ pint
A112X	Casserole with cut glass design	
112	Space Saver clear round casserole	3 pint
113/A113	As 112	2 pint
A113X	Casserole with cut glass	

	design	
122	Space Saver clear oval casserole	1½ pint
125	Space Saver clear oval casserole	2½ pint
128	Space Saver clear oval casserole	4½ pint
130	Divided dish without cover	9¾" x 1 7/8"
130 or 1067	Easy-Grip clear square casserole	2½ pint
132	Pudding dish round (shallow)	
134	Divided dish with cover	9¾" x 1 7/8"
135	Baking dish round (shallow)	
135	Space Saver chicken casserole	
142	Space Saver oblong dish	5 pint
145	Oblong pie dish	1 pint
146	Oblong pie dish	1½ pint
147	Oblong pie dish	2½ pint
155	Pudding dish round (shallow)	
A166B	Pudding dish, round, deep	
A166.5B	Pudding dish	
A167B	Pudding dish	
A168B	Pudding dish	
A169B	Pudding dish	
A170B	Pudding dish	
183B/A183	Pie dish oval shallow	1½ pint

184B/A184	Pie dish oval shallow	2 pint
185B/A185	Pie dish oval shallow	3¼ pint
190B/A190B	Pie dish oval deep	4¼ pt
A191B	Pie dish oval deep	1 pint
192B	Pie dish oval deep	
193B/A193B	Pie dish oval deep	1¾ pint
194B/A194B	Pie dish oval deep	3 pint
197B/A197B	Pie dish oval deep	2¼ pint
TS201	Flameware saucepan	
202	Tart dish narrow rim	
202	Space Saver plate clear	8"
204	Pie plate packed in cartons of 144,12,6	
204	clear plate	9"
205	Pie plate wide rim, round	
S205	Streamline casserole, octagonal	1½ pint
205	Space Saver clear plate	10"
206	Pie plate wide rim	
207	Pie plate wide rim	
208	Pie plate wide rim later 251	
209	Pie plate wide rim	
210	Pie plate wide rim	
212	Bread pan or cake pan oblong	
213	Bread pan or cake pan oblong	
214	Bread pan or cake pan oblong	

218	Space Saver soup bowl clear	
220	Layer cake dish (shallow) round	
221	Cake dish (round)	
230	Space Saver fruit dish clear	
231	Utility dish oblong	
231E	Utility dish, oblong, engraved with floral design	
232	Utility dish oblong	
234	Biscuit pan oblong packed in cartons containing two	9 1/8" x 7 5/8" x 1 ¼ "
235	Biscuit pan oblong	
241	Roasting dish	
250	Flavour saver pie dish, round, later numbered 198	1 pint, 2 pint
260, later 272	Soufflé dish	2¼ pint
A263	Individual casserole packed in cartons of 72,36,12,6	
264	Round casserole – individual casserole	
266/A266	Round casserole	¾ pint
A266X	Casserole with cut glass design	
A266.5	Round casserole	1¼ pint
A266.5X	Casserole with cut glass design	
267/A267	Round casserole	1½ pint
A267 E2	Casserole (round) engraved	

	with flowers	
A2670W	Casserole with willow pattern design	
A267X	Casserole with cut glass design	
S267	Streamline round casserole	
BA2670W	Casserole with blue Willow Pattern design	
268/A268	Round casserole	2¼ pt
A268 E2	casserole (round) engraved with flowers	
A2680W	Casserole with Willow Pattern design	
BA2680W	Casserole with blue Willow Pattern design	
A268X	Cut Glass Casserole Dish	
S268	Streamline casserole, round	2¼ pt
269/A269	Round casserole	3¼ pt
A269 E2	Casserole (round) engraved with flowers	
A2690W	Casserole with Willow Pattern design	
BA2690W	Casserole with blue Willow Pattern design	
A269X	Casserole with cut glass design	
270/A270	Round casserole	4 pint
A270 E2	Casserole (round) engraved with flowers	
A270X	Cut Glass Casserole	
275	Space Saver clear butter dish	
278	Space Saver general purpose dish	2½ pint

283/A283	Oval casserole (shallow) OR entrée dish	1½ pint
A283 E2	Casserole engraved with flowers	
A283X	Casserole with cut glass design	
S283	Streamline casserole, oval	
284/A284	Shallow oval casserole OR entrée dish	2 pint
A284 E2	Casserole engraved with flowers	
A284X	Casserole with cut glass design	
285/A285	Oval casserole (shallow) OR entrée dish	3¼ pt
A285 E2	Casserole engraved with flowers	
A285X	Casserole with cut glass design	
290/A290	Oval casserole (deep) oval	4¼ pt
A290 E2	Oval casserole (deep) engraved with flowers	
A290X	Casserole with cut glass design	
A291	Casserole oval deep	1 pint
A291X	Casserole with cut glass design	
292	Oval casserole (deep) oval	1¼ pt
293/A293	Oval casserole (deep) oval	1¾ pt
A293 E2	Engraved with flowers Oval casserole (deep)	
A293X	Casserole with cut glass design	

294/A294	Oval casserole (deep) oval	3 pint
A294 E2	Oval casserole (deep) engraved with flowers	
A294X	Casserole with cut glass design	
297/A297	Oval casserole (deep)	2¼ pt
A297 E2	Oval casserole (deep) Engraved with flowers	
A297X	Casserole with cut glass design	
300	Au gratin dish small size	
301	Round dish with handles OR eared dish, round	
302	Round dish with handles OR eared dish, round	
313	Fish or meat platter OR oval flat dish	
313E	Platter with engraved floral design	
303 E	Platter engraved with flowers	
303	Mixing bowl, later 184, Colourware	
303W	Platter in willow pattern design	
312	Oval platter, Colourware	12 ¼ "
B313W	Platter in blue Willow Pattern	
314	Fish or meat platter OR oval flat dish	
320	Sauceboat – 241 after 1961	
330	Eared dish oval	
330	Space Saver round casserole	

	set of 3 -1,2,3 pt	
331	Au gratin dish French pattern OR eared dish, oval	
332	Au gratin dish French pattern OR eared dish oval	
350	Soufflé dish, shallow	1pt
351	Soufflé dish shallow	1 3/8 pt
352	Soufflé dish shallow	1¾pt
353	Soufflé dish shallow	2½ pint
360	Soufflé dish deep	1¼ pt
361	Soufflé dish deep	1¾pt
362	Soufflé dish deep	2¼ pt
363	Soufflé dish deep	3pt
382	Colourware plate	7.5"
383	Utility plate	
B383W	Willow Pattern plate	
385	Utility plate later 204	
385W	Utility plate with Willow Pattern	
B385W	Utility plate with blue Willow Pattern	
387	Utility plate	
B387W	Willow Pattern utility plate	
389	Soup plate	
389W	Soup plate in Willow Pattern design	
B389W	Soup plate in blue Willow Pattern design	
390	Colourware soup bowl – elliptical rim handle 217 after	½ pint

	1961	
400	Oval pie dish	
401	Pie dish, oval, packed in cartons of 72,36,12,6	
402	Oval pie dish – packed in cartons containing six	½ pint
403	Oval pie dish	¾ pint
404	Oval pie dish	1¼ pt
405	Oval pie dish	1½ pt
406	Oval pie dish	2 pint
407	Oval pie dish	2½ pt
410 E	Custard cup engraved with flowers	4oz
410	Custard cup	4oz
421	Custard cups or individual baker	
422	Custard cups supplied in sixes	6oz
423	Custard cups supplied in sixes	4oz
423 E	Engraved custard cup, floral design	
424	Custard cups (tall) OR French shape supplied in sixes	4oz
426	Custard cups (tall) OR French shape supplied in sixes	6oz
430 000	Rolling pin with plastic caps	
432	Ramekin, round supplied in sixes	3½ oz
442	Ramekin or individual baker, round supplied in sixes	4oz

450	Pudding dish with tab handles	
452	Individual baking dishes round OR pudding dish	6oz
453	Individual baking dishes round OR pudding dish	8oz
455	Individual baking dishes round OR pudding dish	12oz
463	Pudding dish, round, wide rim	
464	Pudding dish, round, wide rim	
465	Pudding dish, round, wide rim	
466	Pudding dish, round, wide rim	
467	Pudding dish, round, wide rim	
473	Pudding dish round	1½ pt
474	Pudding dish round	1¾ pt
475	Pudding dish round	3pt
480	Scalloped shells	4¼ "
481	Scalloped shells	4¾ "
482	Scalloped shells	6"
500	Individual soup pot or server packed in cartons of 2	7oz
501	Individual opal casserole	
502	Bean pot OR stewpot, round, covered	
502	Refrigerator box, colour sprayed base	

504/A504	Bean pot OR stewpot, round, covered	2 pint
505	Space Saver round casserole dish	1 pint
506/A506	Bean pot OR stewpot, round, covered	3½ pt
509	Space Saver round casserole dish	2 pint
509D	Space Saver Round casserole dish – with stand	2 pint
513	Space Saver Round casserole dish	3 pint
513D	Space Saver Round casserole dish – with stand	3 pint
524	Space Saver Round casserole dish	2.5pt
524D	Space Saver Round casserole dish –with stand	2½ pt
542906	3pt oblong with stand	
533	Pyrex classics hostess casserole, round, with candle warmer stand	
535	Easy roast	
542	Oblong casserole	3 pint
552	Space Saver round casserole	1 ¾ pt
555	Deep round casserole dish	5 pint
600	Plate	6 ½ "
603	Plate	8 ½ "
605	Pie dish, round	1½ pt
611	Oval platter	13"
614	Space Saver soup plate	
620	Cup	

622	Space Saver cup	7oz
625	Saucer	
626	Space Saver saucer	
642	Mushroom dish or savoury dish	
643	Sauceboat and stand, matchmaker	
645	Mushroom dish or savoury dish	
645	Sauceboat and stand, PYREX Royal	
652	Bell cover only, round	
653	Space Saver round plate	6.5"
654	Space Saver round plate	8.5"
655	Space Saver round plate	10"
655	Bell cover only, round	
660	Space Saver shaped plate	12" x 9"
663	Space Saver soup/cereal bowl - eared	
664	Space Saver sauceboat	
665	Space Saver sauceboat stand	
656	Space Saver milk jug	
657	Space Saver sugar bowl	
662	Space Saver fruit dish	
676	Space Saver margarine tub	
677	Sugar basin	
706	Tile OR serving tray or platter, 'useful for serving custard cups or porridge pots. Packed in cartons of 2	
708	Tray OR serving tray or	

	platter	
711	Space Saver butter dish	
726	Round Space Saver casserole set of three	1,2,3 pint
800/A800	Square casserole, covered	2½ pt
800B/A800B	Base of above used as pudding dish (square)	2½ pt
A800 E2	Casserole engraved with flowers	
A800X	Casserole with cut glass design	
904	Space Saver round casserole opal base, tinted cover, opposing curve handles	2½ pt
920	Space Saver plate	6 3/8"
953	Percolator top packed in cartons of 12	1 5/8" rim
954	Percolator top packed in cartons of 12	2 5/22" rim
1040	Easygrip individual casserole	8oz
1041	Easygrip casserole round 103 after 1961	1 pint
1045	Easygrip round casserole, 106 after 1961	2 pint
1067	Easygrip square casserole called 130 after 1961	2½ pt
1101, later 170	Pudding basin	
1105, later 276	Jelly mould	1 pint
1145	Pie dish, oblong	1 pint

1200	EPNS Holder and oval entrée dish (no.283)	2½ pt
1201	EPNS Holder and oval entrée dish (no.283)	2¼ pt
1202	EPNS Holder and oval casserole (no. 297)	
1203	Hexagonal pie plate 'for mince pie etc'	
1205	EPNS Holder and cake dish (no. 221)	
1206	EPNS Holder and oval casserole (no. 294)	
1207	EPNS Holder and round casserole (no. 268)	
1208	EPNS Holder and round casserole (no. 267)	
1209	EPNS Holder and stew pot (no.504)	
1210	EPNS Holder and ramekin (no. 432)	
1211	EPNS Holder and square casserole (no. 800)	
1216	Gift set	
1245	EPNS Holder and utility dish (no. 231)	
1290	Gift set	
	Pyrexette – set of 6 Pyrex dishes in miniature	
1400	Entrée dish lining in Willow Pattern design	
1444	Sauce boat	
1444W	Sauce boat with willow pattern design	

B1444W	Sauce boat in blue Willow Pattern	
1444E	Engraved with flowers sauce boat	
1444X	Sauce boat with cut glass design	
1445	Tumbler cover	
1452	Teapot strainer with special lid	
1464	Sauce boat stand	
1464W	Sauce boat stand with Willow Pattern design	
B1464W	Sauce boat stand in blue Willow Pattern	
1464E	Engraved with flowers sauce boat stand	
1464X	Sauce boat stand with cut glass design	
1473	Soap dish	Diam. 4 5/8"
1480	Fruit bowl, Colourware,	1¾ pt
1481 Later 230	Cereal plate packed in cartons of 144, 72, 3	6oz
1482	Handled ramekin packed in cartons of 144, 72, 3	2¾ oz
1484	Chicken casserole	3½ pt
1484 E2	Engraved pattern chicken casserole	
1484X	Chicken casserole with crisscross cut pattern	
1505	Soup ladle	8"

1519		Large chicken casserole	5 pint
1551		Roasting dish	4 pint
1629		Colourware sauceboat	
1630		Colourware sauceboat stand	
2100 later 620		Opal cup	
2102 later 600		Opal Plate	
2103 later 603		Opal plate	8.52
2104 later 605		Opal plate	10"
2108		Opal hostess set, yellow, red bowls, stand	
2120 later 625		Opal saucer	
2190 later 614		Opal Soup plate	
2130 later 611		Opal Oval platter	
2155 later 640		Opal sauceboat	
2156		Opal sauceboat stand	
S2161		Opal oblong casserole with candle warmer in stand	
2174		Opal mixing bowl set, gaiety gooseberry pink/white	
S2176		Serving bowl, later 679A with candle warmer stand	
S2179		Opal divided veg. dish, oval, with candle warmer stand	
S2184		Opal Easygrip casserole with	2 pint

		clear lid, opposing curve handles, on stand later 506A	
S2187		Opal Easygrip round casserole	3 pint
2188		Opal individual casserole, round later 501	
2190 later 614		Opal soup plate	
2196		Space saver casserole set	
2199		Opal snack server, detachable chrome plated metal wire handle	
2220 later 523		Opal oval casserole	2 ½ pt
2481		Covered butter dish	6¼"
24501		Refrigerator dish	1¼pt
A2670		3 purpose casserole	1½ pt
A2680		3 purpose casserole	2½ pt
A2690		3 purpose casserole	3¾ pt
BA2670W		Streamline casserole with Willow Pattern in blue	
460 028		Juggler coffee jug	1¼pt
490044		Stack-n-store jars (pair)	1lt
491041/1		Stack-n-store jar light or dark brown lid	2lt
		Juggler jugs	1.3 lt
			1lt
			0.7 lt

Bibliography

'*PYREX - 60 Years of Design*'
Tyne and Wear County Council Museums
1983
ISBN 00905974 09 3

'*The 'PYREX' Book of Regional Cookery*'
Diana Cameron-Shea
1977
ISBN 0 09 129 5815

'*PYREX The Unauthorised Collector's* Guide'
Barbara E. Mauzy
2002
ISBN 0 7643 1534 X

www.ingramcontent.com/pod-product-compliance
Lightning Source LLC
Chambersburg PA
CBHW042320150426
43192CB00001B/3